SUICIDE PREVENTION
Hope When Life Seems Hopeless

JUNE HUNT

AspirePress

Torrance, California

CONTENTS

Definitions..9
What Are Different Types of Suicide?..............10
What Are Some Facts
    and Fables about Suicide?....................18

Characteristics.......................................24
What Is the Path of Potential Suicide?............25
What Is the Portrait of Painful Thinking?.......27
What Characterizes Suicidal Teens?................33

Causes...37
Who Is Most Vulnerable to Suicide?..............38
What Do Sufferers Want to Escape?...............39
How Does Fear Relate to Suicide?................44
What Is the Root Cause
    of Suicidal Thinking?......................47
What Is the Source of Hope
    When You've Lost All Hope?..............48

Steps to Solution....................................52
How to Evaluate the Extent
    of the Suicidal Struggle...................54
How to Know the Scriptural
    Reasons to Say No..........................60
How to Be Willing to Be Willing..................63
How to Forgive....................................66
How to Turn from Feeling to Healing..............68
How to Hold On to the Lifeline of Hope..........70
How to Present "The Contract"....................78
How to Connect with Compassion..................83

ear Friend,

I remember the scene like it was yesterday. From my freshman days in college, I still remember my simple question. "*Rosie, are you all right?*"

I had just walked into my dorm room after dinner on campus ... but *something seemed very wrong.* What I saw looked strange at first—then startling. My sweet, joyful roommate was sprawled across her bed, awkwardly angled and glassy-eyed. She did not respond to my question and when I attempted to rouse her, she was like a limp doll.

Instinctively, I looked around the room for any indication of trouble. Sure enough, there was a stash of bottles—*open* bottles—once containing pills. Apparently, this mound of missing pills was all mixed together, dissolving inside Rosie's stomach.

Immediately my heart began to race. Time was of the essence. Her life was in the balance. I ran across the street back to the cafeteria where I had earlier seen my brother, Ray.

"*Please, God, keep him in the cafeteria! Don't let him leave!*" Within moments, I dashed through the tall wooden doorway and then abruptly stopped. "*Lord, help me find him,*" I pleaded.

Scanning the heads of hundreds of students, I stood frozen, feeling as if my heart would beat out of my chest. Finally, spying his short blond hair, I hurried to him and blurted out, "*Rosie attempted suicide! Quick—help me!*"

We rushed back to my dorm and up to the 3rd floor. Scooping her into his arms, Ray carried her out to my car. Driving as fast as I could, we took her to the college health clinic.

The medical staff began pumping Rosie's stomach. I sat in the waiting room and prayed for what seemed like an eternity. Finally a doctor came out and pronounced, *"She's going to make it."* Whew—we made it in time! Thankfully, her life had been saved.

In the wee hours of the morning, I returned to our room *alone*. After collapsing fully clothed on my bed, I began ruminating for over an hour on what had just happened. To begin with, Rosie was the last person I would have linked with suicide. Then I had this realization: Someone I consider a precious friend now seems like a stranger. Here is someone I know and love, and yet I know nothing about the most painful part of her life—the part of her heart that's lost all hope. What could possibly have caused her to want to end her life?

And that led me to another realization: All around us there are people with *hidden pain*—and some have lost all hope. They feel so helpless and hopeless that they're looking for a way to escape.

For many days, Rosie stayed in the clinic recuperating from her overdose and being evaluated by doctors.

Every evening, as I visited her, we would talk for hours. During one of our earlier conversations, I asked, *"Rosie, what has been so painful that you lost your will to live?"* Her answer deeply grieved me, filling my heart with both pain and compassion.

Rosie had experienced the haunting trauma of *childhood sexual abuse*, and the sickening memories had been tormenting her soul. She had suffered alone—she had never told a soul.

But that very evening, she had taken her first step toward healing. She had shared "the secret." The victimizer's power is in manipulating the victim to keep *the secret*. Yet now the secret was out! I also shared her painful truth with a caring, responsible relative—her uncle who was committed to helping Rosie deal with the difficult family dynamics.

Even though her life was saved, there was so much I did not know about helping someone who struggles with suicide. How I wish I'd known *then* what I know *now*. So many struggle with the devastation of feeling *powerless* to stop the pain. Most people who commit suicide don't really want to die; *they just want the pain to stop.*

If you are in such pain, my first words of counsel are, "*Tell someone.*" It's vital that you tell someone what's causing you such pain because only then can hope, help, and healing begin to occur. Jesus says, "*The truth will set you free*" (John 8:32). Plus, you will no longer be alone in your torturous struggle.

Regardless of where you are in your life right now, if God is leading you or preparing you to come alongside a struggler who has lost hope, pray to have the right heart—*God's heart*. His heart is tender and full of compassion toward those experiencing deep pain. The Bible says, "*The LORD longs to be gracious to you; he rises to show you compassion*" (Isaiah 30:18). He feels the emotional, spiritual, and physical agony that engulfs the lives of those teetering on the brink of absolute hopelessness. And from God's tender heart springs forth words of wisdom; life-transforming truths that truly affirm "life."

As you read these words on this significant subject, you will learn how to better reflect God's heart to help those who are hurting, and you will gain practical insight on what to say and what to do. My prayer is that the truths in this book will have a powerful impact in your life, equipping you to literally save the life of someone struggling with thoughts of suicide.

Yours in the Lord's hope,

June

June Hunt

*"There is surely a future hope for you,
and your hope will not be cut off."*
(Proverbs 23:18)

SUICIDE PREVENTION
Hope When Life Seems Hopeless

"I just want to die."

This aching admission has been spoken too many times—and with tragic results. These five words reveal a soul mired in the depths of despair. All hope is gone, and all too soon, so is life itself.

No group is exempt from wanting to walk down this dark path of "escape." Male and female, young and old, rich and poor—all are found among these fatal statistics. Yet most people contemplating suicide don't really want to die—*they just want the pain to stop.* Their burden seems too heavy to bear.

If you're struggling, if you're desperate, if you're contemplating taking your life, realize this: The Lord longs to heal your heart and restore your hope. In absolute honesty, go to God about your pain.

Say to Him ...

**"I am in pain and distress;
may your salvation, O God, protect me."
(Psalm 69:29)**

DEFINITIONS

Does life seem impossible? For over a million people each year who die of suicide, the answer is *yes!* And that figure is more than all the casualties of homicide and war combined![1]

Think about this statistic—seriously: On average, one person dies by suicide every 40 seconds somewhere in the world, while up to 20 others are attempting the same act.[2] That's an extraordinary number of people desperately choosing death!

Have your desires been dashed by the pain of depression and despair? Have your hopes been smashed by hurt and heartache? Have you searched without success for a lasting solution?

Honestly, are you struggling with thoughts of suicide? Have you begun to believe the lie that self-inflicted death would be better than God-given life?

Realize, the Lord looks upon you with tender compassion and genuine concern. He cares about your every need. You can learn how to experience the meaningful life He has planned for you. He has a perfect plan for you; a plan to free you from the shackles of suicidal thinking; a plan based on truth, not on lies. Jesus desires to free you from destructive thoughts and choices. He said ...

> **"You will know the truth,**
> **and the truth will set you free."**
> **(John 8:32)**

Just to hear the word *suicide* evokes a myriad of feelings ranging from shock and sadness to guilt and grief. The initial response after suicide is often: *Oh no! Why would anyone resort to such an irreversible act?*

We feel a sense of tragic loss when we discover that suicide has snuffed out one more life forever. To help someone fight the persistent desire to "end it all" (a desire called suicidal ideation), there is much we need to understand about suicide. Since God is our Creator, we need to know God's heart on life and death—and that means our own life and death. Throughout the Bible, life and death are presented in different contexts, but never does God say we are to pursue death.

> **"I have set before you life and death.
> ... Now choose life, so that you
> and your children may live."
> (Deuteronomy 30:19)**

The Five Sides of Suicide

▶ **Suffering Suicide**

- *Suffering suicide* is a deliberate act of killing oneself while in an extreme state of despair.[4] (In Latin, *sui* means "oneself" and *cide* means "to kill.")

- Suicidal sufferers are afflicted with "tunnel vision"—the only option they see is death. They cannot see any hope that their painful life will be any different in the future.

BIBLICAL EXAMPLE: Judas hanged himself in remorse after betraying Jesus.

"When Judas, who had betrayed him, saw that Jesus was condemned, he was seized with remorse. ... Then he went away and hanged himself." (Matthew 27:3, 5)

▶ Supported Suicide

- *Supported suicide* (also called "assisted suicide") is a deliberate choice of killing oneself with the assistance of another person.

- Supported suicide (sometimes referred to by terms like "euthanasia" or "mercy killing") is an attempt to avoid a painful or undesirable future.

BIBLICAL EXAMPLE: The evil king Abimelech asked his soldier to kill him with a sword in order to avoid the humiliation of military defeat. This hurried request to his armor-bearer was for "assisted suicide."

"Draw your sword and kill me, so that they can't say, 'A woman killed him.' So his servant ran him through, and he died." (Judges 9:54)

▶ Symbolic Suicide

- *Symbolic suicide* is a deliberate act of killing oneself while being influenced by a ritualistic custom or a sense of honor due to an excessive identification with a certain person, family, or nation.

- Symbolic suicide is found in different cultures and enacted in different ways. Types of symbolic suicide include hara-kiri, suttee, and copycat suicides.

HISTORICAL EXAMPLES:

- *Hara-kiri* (*hara* means "belly" and *kiri* means "cutting") is the Japanese ritual of "honorable suicide" by ripping open the abdomen with a knife (disembowelment) in response to bringing dishonor on one's family.

- *Suttee* (also *Sati*) is the Hindu custom of a widow cremating herself on her husband's funeral pyre to demonstrate her ultimate act of fidelity. This practice can be either voluntary or compulsory, depending on where the widow lives. Today in India, suttee is forbidden by law, although some widows still choose this suicidal act, and still others are pressured to do so.

BIBLICAL EXAMPLE: After regaining his supernatural strength, Samson—one of Israel's judges— pushed against the temple's two central pillars, knowing he would be killed. But he also knew the collapse would kill the Philistines—the enemy of God and His people.

"Samson reached toward the two central pillars on which the temple stood. Bracing himself against them, his right hand on the one and his left hand on the other, Samson said, 'Let me die with the Philistines!' Then he pushed with all his might, and down came the temple on the rulers and all the people in it. Thus he killed many more when he died than while he lived." (Judges 16:29–30)

▶ Shared Suicide

- *Shared suicide* is the deliberate act of two or more people who kill themselves based on a prior commitment to do so.

- Suicide pacts are previously arranged deaths that typically take place at the same time, for the same cause, using the same method.

HISTORICAL EXAMPLE: In AD 70 after Rome destroyed Jerusalem and the temple, the Jews were taken captive and many were dispersed to other nations. However, around 960 zealots escaped to Masada, a fortress situated on a massive isolated rock 900 feet high. In AD 73 the Jews of Masada knew their stronghold could not withstand the overpowering Roman siege. Rather than allow their wives and children to be tortured, abused, or sold as slaves, they chose to die of mass suicide.[5]

Knowing that these Jewish zealots were well acquainted with the Psalms, no doubt they could identify with these words:

"The cords of death entangled me, the anguish of the grave came upon me; I was overcome by trouble and sorrow." (Psalm 116:3)

▶ Slaughter Suicide

- *Slaughter suicide* is the deliberate act of killing one or more people while committing suicide simultaneously or immediately following the act of murder.

- Slaughter suicide is called "homicidal suicide," which includes killings committed by groups such as kamikaze pilots and suicide bombers.

13

HISTORICAL EXAMPLES:

- *Jihad suicide bombers* seek to fulfill the Islamic directive in the Qur'an against all non-Islamic people: "Fight and slay the Pagans wherever ye find them, and seize them, beleaguer them, and lie in wait for them in every stratagem (of war) ... Fight those who believe not in Allah" (Surah 9:5, 29). Those who die as jihadists are "guaranteed" their place in paradise (along with 70 of their relatives), bypassing the normally required time in hell, and they are given 72 virgins to enjoy.

- *Kamikaze* ("divine wind") *pilots* in Japan carried out their suicide missions during World War II by flying their war planes into enemy targets such as ships and ammunition depots. These pilots believed they were guaranteed a place with their ancestors and believed their highest service was to die for the Emperor who was regarded as God. (In 1945, following the Japanese defeat, the Emperor pronounced on the radio, "I am no longer to be considered a deity.")

CULTURAL EXAMPLE: On Tuesday April 20, 1999—in celebration of Hitler's birthday—two sadistic high school students in long, black trench coats killed thirteen people at Columbine High School in Littleton, Colorado. After the hate-filled massacre—especially targeting Christians—they both committed suicide. Known as cruel bullies, these two killers lived out this Scripture:

"Bloodthirsty men hate a man of integrity and seek to kill the upright." (Proverbs 29:10)

Bully-Cide

QUESTION: "What is 'bully-cide'?"

ANSWER: *Bully-cide* refers to a person who dies of suicide because of the torment, fear, and humiliation associated with being bullied. Immature children are notorious for picking on one another. However, today's bullies are far more cruel than in previous generations because, in addition to bullying their victims at school and in other social settings, home provides no haven of refuge for those being bullied. These bullies use their cell phones and computers to attack their human targets at all hours of the day and night. It's virtually impossible for victims to find a sense of safety anywhere unless they isolate themselves and abandon the use of phones and computers. With no reprieve from the constant barrage of bullying, these victims feel so belittled and besieged that eventually they:

▶ Lose their ability to function normally

▶ Experience mental and emotional symptoms similar to those who are being terrorized

▶ Suffer plummeted self-worth and impaired resilience

▶ Endure such degradation and scorn that some believe suicide is their only viable option

▶ Could opt for killing their bullies rather than themselves—or even both

Unless some observant, wise person recognizes their symptoms and intervenes in their lives in a powerful, caring way, there is little hope for these strugglers. Parents, educators, and coaches need to take action on behalf of those being bullied. This biblical passage could not be more relevant:

> **"Rescue those being led away to death; hold back those staggering toward slaughter. If you say, 'But we knew nothing about this,' does not he who weighs the heart perceive it?**
> **Does not he who guards your life know it? Will he not repay each person according to what he has done?"**
> **(Proverbs 24:11–12)**

Copycat Suicides

"Copycats" are people who imitate the behaviors of others and sometimes this imitation extends to the realm of suicide. The intent of a copycat is to make the ultimate sacrifice—believing that one's own self-imposed death will bring honor to another person's life.

▶ **Copycat suicides** are intentionally self-inflicted deaths due to the desire to imitate others who have killed themselves. Copycats most often commit suicide following the death of people in three categories: friends, family, and the famous (specifically friends/classmates, siblings/parents, heroes/idols).

▶ **Celebrity suicides** spawn multiple suicide attempts because the copycat feels such a strong sense of identification with the celebrity—even a part of the celebrity's fame. After the celebrity's death, copycat suicides tend to occur at specific intervals:

- Within the first three days
- On the one week, one month, or one year anniversaries
- On the same day of the month (such as the 4th or 11th)

▶ **Cluster suicides** involve a group of people who so identify with someone's suicide that they feel compelled to identify with that person in death. These suicides take place together in a group or separately at the same time.

- They may fantasize hovering over and watching their own funerals.
- They may idealize their deaths as "honoring" the one whom they are imitating.
- They may romanticize how much their own suicides would affect others, imagining the tears of those left behind, their words of guilt and regret, the sorrow of how much they will be missed.

Tragically, copycats fail to realize that the far greater way to honor someone is through life, not death, by living in a way that honors the memory of the one who has died, not by dying in a way that brings only a brief moment of fame. Be aware of those who are immature and impressionable; those who don't have a secure sense of their own identity; those who lack judgment by fantasizing about and romanticizing suicide. In general, the Bible addresses this basic tragedy:

> **"Fools die for lack of judgment."**
> **(Proverbs 10:21)**

WHAT ARE Some Facts and Fables about Suicide?

Consider him Australia's *Dr. Death.*

Not only has Dr. Philip Nitschke conducted *how-to-commit suicide* classes, he developed the "peaceful pill"—a drug he claims will serenely usher in death—a drug he designed to be on grocery store shelves. And even more chilling is one of the markets targeted for his death drug: troubled teens known to be highly impressionable and immature. He states ...

> *My personal position is that if we believe that there is a right to life, and then we must accept that people have a right to dispose of that life whenever they want. ... And someone needs to provide this knowledge, training, or resource necessary to anyone who wants it, including the depressed, the elderly bereaved, the troubled teen.*[6] [sic]

What you believe about suicide is critical. Your thoughts about suicide will shape your response. You need wisdom to discern what is false and what is true about self-imposed death. The wisdom of God's Word will help you know how to have the right response.

> **"The teaching of the wise is**
> **a fountain of life, turning a man**
> **from the snares of death."**
> **(Proverbs 13:14)**

#1 FABLE: "Never talk about suicide with deeply depressed people—it could give them ideas."[7]

▶ **FACT:** Asking about what someone is feeling doesn't create suicidal thoughts. You can assume that most depressed or very anxious people have given some thought to taking their lives. Demystify the subject by talking about suicide. Ask questions such as:

- "What do you think about suicide?"

- "Do your friends talk about it?"

- "Do you know anyone who has died of suicide?"

- "Would you ever take your own life?"

▶ For a person considering suicide, having someone to talk with can be a powerful preventive. The Bible says ...

"The wise in heart are called discerning, and pleasant words promote instruction." (Proverbs 16:21)

#2 FABLE: "People who talk about killing themselves never do it."

▶ **FACT:** Of those who took their own lives, approximately 75% gave clues or warnings to friends or family. Take any threat of suicide seriously. Someone who talks about suicide gives others the opportunity to intervene. God's Word says ...

"Be completely humble and gentle; be patient, bearing with one another in love." (Ephesians 4:2)

#3 FABLE: "More suicides occur during the winter holidays."

▶ FACT: This is a long-standing myth; however, suicides are actually lowest in December. In general:[8]

- Suicide rates are below average in the winter and above average in the spring, peaking in April.

- For youth, suicide rates are higher in the summer.

- For middle-aged adults age 36 and up, suicide rates rise again in the fall.

- In general, suicide risks decrease as social interactions increase. Becoming aware of the most frequent occurrences of suicide will help you discern when a struggler is at risk.

"The heart of the discerning acquires knowledge; the ears of the wise seek it out." (Proverbs 18:15)

#4 FABLE: "Talking about the method of someone's suicide with all the gory details and the emotional impact on loved ones will help prevent others from committing suicide."

▶ FACT: Presenting precise details of a suicide, including the heartbreaking reaction of the family, can spark an explosion of copycat suicides. School officials and people in the media have learned that suicide can be contagious; therefore, they curtail details of *what* happened and instead focus on *why* it happened as a preventative. "Suicide contagion"[9] refers to suicidal behavior on the part of vulnerable people who can be easily influenced to commit suicide because of a previous attempt or another's death. The Bible often gives warning about the misuse of our words.

"There is ... a time to be silent and a time to speak." (Ecclesiastes 3:1, 7)

#5 FABLE: "Everyone who commits suicide is mentally ill."

▶ **FACT:** No, not everyone. Of those who kill themselves, approximately 90% are afflicted with a diagnosable psychiatric disorder.[10] However, look at the life of Elijah; he was terrified and wanted to die.

"Elijah was afraid and ran for his life. ... [He] prayed that he might die. 'I have had enough, LORD,' he said. 'Take my life.'" (1 Kings 19:3–4)

#6 FABLE: "Suicidal tendencies are inherited."

▶ **FACT:** No one is destined to die of suicide. Just because one family member dies by suicide doesn't mean that other family members will do the same. However, be aware:

- Based on statistical data, those with depressed family members are two times more vulnerable to depression than those who have no family history of depression. Likewise, "50% of manic-depressives have at least one parent with the disorder."[11] Untreated depression can lead to suicide.

- Suicide can also be a "learned behavior" that is passed down through family environment. For example, the Bible reveals in numerous places that the sins of our fathers can be repeated by successive generations.

"He committed all the sins his father had done before him; his heart was not fully devoted to the Lord his God." (1 Kings 15:3)

#7 Fable: "Suicide is the unpardonable sin."

▶ **Fact:** Nowhere in the Bible is suicide presented as the unpardonable sin. The unpardonable sin is the unwillingness to yield to the convicting work of the Holy Spirit, which leads to salvation through Jesus Christ.

"Whoever blasphemes against the Holy Spirit will never be forgiven; he is guilty of an eternal sin." (Mark 3:29)

#8 Fable: "Christians who take their own lives lose their salvation."

▶ **Fact:** According to the Word of God, once you have believed in and relied on Christ as your Lord and Savior, you have the promised *guarantee* from the Spirit of God, who is deposited in you, that you will inherit heaven and live eternally in the presence of God.

"You also were included in Christ when you heard the word of truth, the gospel of your salvation. Having believed, you were marked in him with a seal, the promised Holy Spirit, who is a deposit guaranteeing our inheritance until the redemption of those who are God's possession." (Ephesians 1:13–14)

#9 FABLE: "Deeply committed believers would never want to commit suicide."

▶ **FACT:** Temporary hopelessness can accompany severe stress and can strain a person's faith. Likewise, physical illnesses, such as a brain tumor, can change thought processes in the brain, resulting in "suicidal ideation." Even the most sincere believer can become engulfed in suicidal despair. When the godly prophet Jeremiah was tormented and his life threatened, he lamented ...

"Cursed be the day I was born! May the day my mother bore me not be blessed! ... Why did I ever come out of the womb to see trouble and sorrow and to end my days in shame?" (Jeremiah 20:14–18)

#10 FABLE: "Once people attempt suicide, they will always be weak and unable to face difficulties in life."

▶ **FACT:** In the context of a person's whole life, a true crisis usually lasts for only a brief duration of time. Most people learn valuable life lessons during their lowest moments. God rescues from destruction those who turn to Him for His love and acceptance. This is clearly seen in the life of Isaiah.

"Surely it was for my benefit that I suffered such anguish. In your love you kept me from the pit of destruction; you have put all my sins behind your back." (Isaiah 38:17)

CHARACTERISTICS

He's soared to the heights—and plunged to the depths.

He's known exhilaration—and felt exhaustion. Tony Dungy coached the Indianapolis Colts to victory in Super Bowl XLI, a feat doubly honored because he was the first African-American coach to win football's premier event watched by millions around the world. But Dungy has also experienced loss—painful loss, grievous loss—and not just the kind played on the football field.[12]

The coach's oldest son, Jamie, took his own life.

"I just wish he would have made it to 20," said Jamie's sister.[13] Tiara believed that teenage rebellion played a large role in her brother's suicide. Once he began defying parental guidance, he also started veering off the path—the straight path that had provided stability.

Of course, that guidance would have made much more sense as he matured, but Jamie died at age 18. And the parental advice Jamie once sought and heeded became marred by the mixed messages he received from the world. Jamie would have escaped his early death had he heeded this wise counsel:

**"Listen, my son, accept what I say,
and the years of your life will be many."
(Proverbs 4:10)**

Every sheep needs a shepherd. It's a life-and-death matter. When a sheep crosses a stream, if its wool coat becomes saturated with water, the top-heavy sheep topples over. The sheep is said to be "cast down." Without the aid of a shepherd, this sheep literally cannot stand up. Soon the sheep will die.

If you become so heavy-laden that you fall with the weight you are carrying, you too need the Shepherd—you need a strong hand to help you up—for it, too, could be a matter of life or death for you. The psalmist, who clearly understood tragedy and despair, wrote these graphic words:

> **"Why are you downcast, O my soul?**
> **Why so disturbed within me?**
> **Put your hope in God, for I will yet praise**
> **him, my Savior and my God."**
> **(Psalm 42:11)**

Be aware of the three stages of being "cast down."[14]

Three Stages of Potential Suicide

1 DOWNCAST: Early Stage

- Dejection
- Change in eating and sleeping habits
- Avoidance of family
- Decline in work or school performance
- Anxiety
- Inability to concentrate or make decisions

25

- Boredom

- Lack of interest in the future

"I remember my affliction and my wandering, the bitterness and the gall. I well remember them, and my soul is downcast within me." (Lamentations 3:19–20)

2 DISTRESSED: Advanced Stage

- Depression

- Withdrawal from family and friends

- Rapid mood swings

- Physical problems, self injury, anorexia

- Self-pity

- Excessive absences from work or school

- Either apathy or anger

- Neglect of personal appearance

"Trouble and distress have come upon me. ... Be merciful to me, O Lord, for I am in distress; my eyes grow weak with sorrow, my soul and my body with grief." (Psalm 119:143; Psalm 31:9)

3 DESPAIRING: Danger Stage

- Hopelessness

- Giving away personal possessions

- Deep remorse

- Suicidal threats or previous attempts

- Abusing alcohol/drugs

- Organizing personal affairs: making a will, paying off debts

- Isolation or morose behavior

- Sudden change from depression to cheerfulness (being at peace with the decision of suicide)

"The cords of the grave coiled around me; the snares of death confronted me." (2 Samuel 22:6)

Note: If you are experiencing any of these physical or emotional problems, be sure to consult your health care professional.

WHAT IS the Portrait of Painful Thinking?

Rarely does a person choose the act of suicide on an impulse. Friends and family often think the loss of their loved one resulted from an isolated moment of despair. Yet suicide usually occurs after a long process of destructive thinking and clouded conclusions are left unchecked. These faulty thoughts lead to a denial of truth and a disconnection with people. A common thought is, *No one understands me, no one feels the way I do.*

Everyone has struggled with discouragement. Everyone has wrestled with their thoughts, even God's appointed king, David.

"How long must I wrestle with my thoughts and every day have sorrow in my heart? How long will my enemy triumph over me?" (Psalm 13:2)

Suicidal Thinking of the Sufferer

▶ "There is nothing left in life that I care about. It's pointless to go on living."

▶ "I can't face the future. The only thing to do is escape."

▶ "Things will never change. Death would be better than this."

▶ "I don't amount to anything. I may as well end it all."

▶ "My life is completely out of control. I'll have to get the upper hand."

▶ "It won't really hurt anyone else. Actually, I will be doing everyone a favor."

▶ "I've done all that can be done. There is only one thing left to do."

▶ "Soon it will be all over, and then I will have peace!"

▶ "I can't go on living like this. Life is hopeless."

▶ "I'm too depressed to go on. When I'm gone I won't have to deal with it."

▶ "You'll be sorry when I'm gone."

▶ "I need Jesus in my life. I'll go to heaven and be with Him forever."

▶ "I can take a small amount of 'this' to see how it feels; then I can add more."

▶ "Everyone will understand. I have suffered long enough."

▶ "Everyone has given up on me, so I'm giving up on me!"

▶ "If I continue with this negative behavior, they'll be glad to see me go."

▶ "It made him famous; maybe it'll make me famous too!"

▶ "It hurts so much! I am really going to do it ... but please stop me."

▶ "If I continue to talk about it, it will not be a surprise and will not hurt them as much."

▶ "You say I talk about suicide just for attention. I will show you!"

Those who have lost hope finally come to the conclusion that death is the only logical solution to their problems. But this is a lie. *Suicide is never the answer—getting help is the answer.* God knows the pressure you are under. Let that pressure press you closer to the Shepherd of your soul. You, and all other sufferers, can verbally claim these words:

**"We are hard pressed on every side, but not crushed; perplexed, but not in despair; persecuted, but not abandoned; struck down, but not destroyed."
(2 Corinthians 4:8–9)**

Helping a Suicidal Parent

QUESTION: "What could help a parent reject suicide?"

ANSWER: Most parents take seriously the role of "provider/protector" for their children. Therefore, this logical series of questions could help bring a suicidal parent out of the emotional abyss.

▶ "What ages are your children?"

▶ "Do you love your children?"

▶ "Do you *really* love your children?"

▶ "How *much* do you love them?"

▶ "Tell me what you love about your children."

▶ "Do you care about their hearts?"

▶ "How would they feel if you were gone?"

▶ "Do you really want your children to grow up without a father/mother?"

▶ "How do you imagine your children would feel if you weren't there for their significant events—graduations, weddings, birth of grandchildren?"

▶ "Do you really want your children to feel abandoned for the rest of their lives?"

▶ "While suicide seems the way to get rid of your pain, it actually transfers your pain to those who love you. So would you be willing to let your fatherly/motherly love protect your children from that pain?"

Realize that those who die by suicide weigh their loved ones down with the heaviest burden of pain possible, leaving them wounded and scarred with the possibility of becoming bitter and deeply discouraged. The Bible says ...

> **"Do not embitter your children,**
> **or they will become discouraged."**
> **(Colossians 3:21)**

Read this verse every day, pray for God's healing, and focus your mind on the reality that ...

> **"Children's children are a crown**
> **to the aged, and parents are**
> **the pride of their children."**
> **(Proverbs 17:6)**

Helping a Suicidal Husband

QUESTION: **"What could help a husband reject suicide?"**

ANSWER: One approach is to encourage him to think through the logical, probable impact of suicide on his wife by asking him a progression of questions.

▶ "Have you thought about how you would take your life?"

- "I'd probably shoot myself."

▶ "Then what would happen?"

- "I guess someone would find me."

31

▶ "Then what?"

- "They'd probably call the police."

▶ "Then what?"

- "The police would contact my wife."

▶ "Then what would happen?"

- "My wife would go to pieces!"

▶ "So, why haven't you done this before now?"

- "I don't want my wife to go to pieces. I don't want to devastate her."

If you can get the struggler to reason through the devastating repercussion on his wife by using this series of questions, then you are well on your way to helping him save his life. You are in a position to help him find a real solution to his painful situation. You could also share these verses compassionately.

"Husbands ought to love their wives as their own bodies. He who loves his wife loves himself. ... Each one of you also must love his wife as he loves himself."
(Ephesians 5:28, 33)

The husband does not have the right to destroy what is considered one body in God's eyes.

"They are no longer two, but one. Therefore what God has joined together, let man not separate."
(Matthew 19:6)

Every creation of God is unique—a one-of-a-kind masterpiece. That's one reason most people are shocked to learn that suicide is the sixth leading cause of death among children who are 5–14 years old.

Tragically, suicide is the third leading cause of death for 15–24-year-olds.[15] Teenagers who are emotionally vulnerable to suicide react excessively to mild stress and react longer than usual after the stress has lessened. They feel more deeply than other teens and then hold on to those feelings for a longer period of time. This means any negative thoughts of low self-worth or self-hatred become an explosive powder keg for destructive behavior.

The wisdom and compassion of Ecclesiastes 7:17 can be shared with teenagers: *"Do not be a fool— why die before your time?"*

The following list characterizes teens who are more vulnerable to suicide than the average teen, although all teens are vulnerable to fleeting thoughts of suicide.

▶ **Behaviors**

- *Impulsive* (using drugs or alcohol, acting out sexually, going on gambling or spending sprees, binge eating or not eating, engaging in other risk-taking behaviors on a dare or without weighing the consequences)

- *Self-injury* (transferring unmanageable emotional pain into manageable physical pain, using physical pain to displace emotional numbness, or incurring bodily injury to cause the brain to naturally release mood-elevating endorphins in order to feel better)

▶ **Emotions**

- *Moody* (switching rapidly between feeling angry, sad, calm, fearful, or happy with little provocation)

- *Reactive* (having little control over lengthy extreme emotional responses of anger, agitation, frustration, sadness, hopelessness, or happiness)

▶ **Relationships**

- *Unpredictable* (switching from being loving to loathsome, smothering to snubbing, clinging to caustic, distant to demanding, hospitable to hostile, responsive to rejecting, and sensitive to stoic)

- *Unstable* (continually feeling misunderstood, emotionally empty, needlessly anxious, and either fearful of abandonment or scared of enmeshment)

▶ **Thoughts**

- *Illogical* (forming beliefs about God, people, and situations not based on reality; the imagined fear of being alone, unloved, or abandoned; and dissociating under extreme stress)

- *Distrustful* (questioning the truthfulness of others, espousing black and white thinking, expecting to be betrayed, deserted, and left all alone)

▶ **Spirituality**

- *Legalistic* (trying to earn God's approval, viewing Him as uninvolved and removed emotionally, spiritually, and physically)

- *Conflicted* (perceiving God as either friend or foe, judge or just, vacillating between loving Him and fearing Him or accepting Him and rejecting Him)

▶ **Self**

  - *Poor Self-image* (having no clear sense of self apart from others, taking on the values and characteristics of companions, emulating a peer group, comparing all aspects of self to others, and being highly sensitive to others)

  - *Low Self-esteem* (feeling lost and lonely when not around others; having self-doubt and self-hatred; being indecisive and insecure, unable to identify or express personal feelings, wants, desires, goals, likes and dislikes, but highly aware of others' feelings, etc.)

Vulnerable adolescents are highly emotional, and unless they learn to manage their impulsive overreactions, they are likely to be controlled by them. The challenge these adolescents face is formidable, but definitely not impossible.

The One who created every part of them longs that they totally rely on Him so that He can pour His peace into them. Only the God of hope can fill the heart with such inner peace that it will naturally overflow with lasting hope. The Bible says ...

"May the God of hope fill you with all joy and peace as you trust in him, so that you may overflow with hope by the power of the Holy Spirit."
(Romans 15:13)

Self-Injury and Suicide

QUESTION: "Are 'cutters'—those who intentionally and repeatedly cut themselves—trying to commit suicide?"

ANSWER: Usually not. Typically, those who practice repeated self-harming behaviors—cutting, burning, biting, scratching, reopening barely healed wounds, etc.—have no intention of dying. Instead, they are seeking relief from their overwhelming emotional pain. They temporarily feel a release of tension and/or shame when they self-injure.

▶ Many strugglers engage in self-harm for additional reasons, such as to self-punish, to stop dissociation (DID), to receive special attention, or to experience euphoria when endorphins are released during self-injury.

▶ Strugglers who harm themselves may become suicidal if the self-injury no longer provides short-term relief from their pain. Since self-injury can be a prelude to suicide, a professional should determine the degree of risk.

These strugglers need to know on a very deep level that they don't have to shed their blood to relieve their emotional pain because Jesus has already given His life for them. The Bible says ...

> "You were redeemed ...
> with the precious blood of Christ,
> a lamb without blemish or defect."
> (1 Peter 1:18–19)

CAUSES

Anger. Sadness. Despair. Grief.

Of all the emotions associated with suicide, hopelessness is the most predominant—the painful feeling that signals for far too many that it's time to give up.

To those who have lost hope, the faulty assumptions are: *My future holds no promise. My wrongs won't be forgiven. My dreams won't come true.* So goes the fatalistic thinking of the hopeless.

But God has a message to those who feel so miserable: "Put your hope in Me, the One who is sovereign over all of your future; the One who can forgive your mistakes; the One who has a purpose and a plan for you."

As long as there is still breath in your body, there is still time for God to dramatically turn your life around. The Bible says ...

"Anyone who is among the living has hope."
(Ecclesiastes 9:4)

It's a grim statistic that should move every one of us into action when we hear someone seriously alluding to suicide. According to the World Health Organization, almost 3,000 people around the world die by suicide daily, while between 30,000 to 60,000 more people attempt to take their own lives.[16]

Actually, suicide is a secondary response, meaning suicide is a behavior that is a response to a deeper problem. Therefore, we need to be aware of how to help suicidal people handle their deeper problems. Realize one day God may call on you to step in and stop a person on the verge of suicide.

> **"Now about brotherly love we do not need to write to you, for you yourselves have been taught by God to love each other. ...**
> **Yet we urge you, brothers,**
> **to do so more and more."**
> **(1 Thessalonians 4:9–10)**

▶ Suicide attempts are more likely within the first year after an unsuccessful attempt.[17]

▶ Suicide rates are higher in sparsely populated areas.[18]

▶ Suicide rates are higher among those who are single, separated, divorced, or widowed.[19]

▶ Suicide rates are highest among white men over 75 years of age.[20]

▶ Suicide is the second leading cause of death for people 10 to 24 years of age.[21]

▶ Suicide occurs more often among nonreligious people than among those who have a strong belief in God.[22]

WHAT DO Sufferers Want to Escape?

The most predominant method of suicide in the United States is the use of firearms. Among Asian countries, poisoning by pesticides is prevalent along with the emergence of a new method called "charcoal-burning." (Charcoal is burned in a sealed-off, confined area, and victims die from carbon monoxide poisoning.) Ingesting drugs is common in Nordic countries and in the United Kingdom. The most often practiced form of suicide worldwide, however, is hanging.[23]

How staggering to grasp that for all the multiple millions who have ever taken their lives, not once has suicide been the will of God. *Not once!* God longs to help, to heal, and to make whole again the broken lives and shattered hearts. The desire of the Lord is to restore lives through His love and give comfort and compassion. Every struggler can pray these words from the Psalms.

"May your unfailing love be my comfort. ...
Let your compassion come
to me that I may live."
(Psalm 119:76–77)

Shooting, hanging, and drug overdoses have traditionally been the most common methods of suicide. Now a dangerous new trend has emerged that also puts others at risk. Producing and inhaling the highly poisonous hydrogen sulfide gas, made from a combination of household products, can endanger people throughout an entire building.[24]

Such desperate acts raise the question, "Why?" What could possibly lead people to endanger the lives of others? What are they so determined to escape? Suicide is a desperate attempt to get out of what seems to be an intolerable situation. It appears to be a way of escape from the pain of living.[25] But the Bible says ...

**"Our God is a God who saves; from the Sovereign LORD comes escape from death."
(Psalm 68:20)**

The Great ESCAPE

The following is an acrostic of the word ESCAPE.

Excessive Loss

- Loss of employment

- Loss of loved one to suicide

- Loss of finances

- Loss of reputation

- Loss of goals

- Loss of romantic love

- Loss of intact family

- Loss of spouse

Social Isolation

- Feeling abandoned
- Feeling unaccepted by family
- Feeling insignificant
- Feeling uninvolved in social activities
- Feeling unloved
- Feeling unimportant to others
- Feeling unnecessary
- Feeling disconnected from God

Critical Illness/Impairment

- Chronic pain
- Major surgery
- Chronic depression
- Physical disability
- Debilitating illness
- Terminal illness

Abusive Background

- Alcohol/drug abuse
- Physical abuse
- Emotional abuse
- Sexual abuse
- Mental abuse
- Spiritual abuse

- Verbal abuse

- Satanic/ritual abuse

Psychological Disorders

Over 90% of people who die by suicide have a mental disorder.[26] Untreated depression can significantly increase the risk for suicide. (A disorder is a psychological condition whereby normal activities of daily living are impaired.)

▶ Chemical imbalance

- Postpartum Depression

- Substance-Induced Psychotic Disorder

▶ Anxiety disorders

- Panic disorders

- Post-Traumatic Stress Disorder

▶ Clinical depression

- Unipolar Depression

- Bipolar Depression

▶ Neurosis (mental and emotional instability without hallucinations or delusions)

- Borderline Personality Disorder

- Eating disorders (anorexia, bulimia)

▶ Dissociative disorders

- Dissociative Identity Disorder (Multiple Personality Disorder)

- Amnesia disorders

▶ Psychosis (break with reality with hallucinations and/or delusions)

- Schizophrenia

- Delusional disorders

EXCESSIVE GUILT

- Extreme remorse over sin

- Perfectionism (performance-based acceptance)

- Failure to meet unrealistic expectations

- Shame or feeling defective

- Legalistic religion

- Unnatural sexual deviations

If you feel trapped in torment, you must refuse to focus on suicide. Your true escape is to see the Lord as your Savior. As you release all of your pain to the Redeemer—each hurt, each pain, each care—He will, in turn, release you from being entrapped in suicidal desires.

> **"My eyes are ever on the LORD, for only**
> **he will release my feet from the snare."**
> **(Psalm 25:15)**

When someone we know has been suicidal, we typically feel a strong sense of sadness. In fact, our feelings can run the gamut of emotions from frustration to fear, from hurt to helplessness. The emotional impact can be overwhelming.

Likewise, those who contemplate suicide also experience different types of emotions prior to their attempts. Although Scripture does not specifically use the word *suicide*, it does describe the emotional state of those who choose suicide.

Most suicides are caused by a psychiatric disorder—a physical condition in the brain—but other causes can be based on severely stressful situations. While emotions vary, a common contributor to a "suicidal crisis" is a sense of overwhelming fear of a situation—a dreaded expectation of impending doom. Those who feel such emotions today can easily identify with these words from Scripture:

**"Fear and trembling have beset me;
horror has overwhelmed me."
(Psalm 55:5)**

The Bible describes many people so overcome with fear that they resort to suicide. These suicidal scenarios reveal:

▶ **Fear of extreme pain, abuse, or torture**

Example: King Saul, was afraid of torture following his military defeat.

"Saul said to his armor-bearer, 'Draw your sword and run me through, or these uncircumcised fellows will come and abuse me.' But his armor-bearer was terrified and would not do it; so Saul took his own sword and fell on it." (1 Chronicles 10:4)

▶ **Fear of being left behind**

Example: King Saul's armor-bearer was terrified following the death of his leader.

"When the armor-bearer saw that Saul was dead, he too fell on his sword and died." (1 Chronicles 10:5)

▶ **Fear of repercussions**

Example: Ahithophel had ignited mutiny against David.

"When Ahithophel saw that his advice had not been followed. ... He put his house in order and then hanged himself." (2 Samuel 17:23)

▶ **Fear of humiliation**

Example: King Abimelech was afraid that a mere woman would kill him.

"'Draw your sword and kill me, so that they can't say, "A woman killed him."' So his servant ran him through, and he died." (Judges 9:54)

▶ **Fear of retaliation and murder**

Example: Zimri had committed many evils.

"When Zimri saw that the city was taken, he ... set the palace on fire around him. So he died, because of the sins he had committed, doing evil in the eyes of the LORD." (1 Kings 16:18–19)

▶ **Fear of severe punishment**

Example: The Philippian jailer, thinking he had failed at his job, feared he would be killed.

"The jailer woke up, and when he saw the prison doors open, he drew his sword and was about to kill himself because he thought the prisoners had escaped. But Paul shouted, 'Don't harm yourself! We are all here!'" (Acts 16:27–28)

Since fear is a powerful catalyst, when you first have thoughts of suicide, take this proverb to heart:

**"Fear of man will prove to be a snare,
but whoever trusts in the LORD is kept safe."
(Proverbs 29:25)**

Life seems dark, hopeless, and purposeless for suicidal strugglers. But the Lord plans for each person to experience His light of life. God created everyone with an inner need to feel significant, yet the desire to live slowly burns out within a heart that no longer sees a reason to live. As the candle of hope is extinguished, that inner sense of purpose is snuffed out by overwhelming despair. One day, however, you too can say what the psalmist said to God:

> **"You have delivered me from death
> and my feet from stumbling,
> that I may walk before God in the
> light of life." (Psalm 56:13)**

WRONG BELIEF:

"I feel like my life is hopeless—I just want to die. I see no purpose in living."

RIGHT BELIEF:

"I'm choosing to walk by faith, not by sight. Instead of letting my feelings control me, I'm letting Christ control me. I'm placing my hope in the Lord, knowing He has a plan and purpose for my life."

> **"'I know the plans I have for you,'
> declares the LORD, 'plans to prosper you and
> not to harm you, plans to give you
> hope and a future.'" (Jeremiah 29:11)**

In the life and death battle for every person on earth, Satan criticizes while Jesus calls. Satan criticizes to dash hope and to destroy while Jesus calls to restore hope and to heal.

Jesus calls Himself *"the good shepherd,"* compassionately nurturing His sheep and sacrificing for them, even to the point of laying down His own life on their behalf. Jesus describes Satan as *"the thief,"* whose only concern is killing, stealing, and destroying. Jesus said, *"The thief comes only to steal and kill and destroy. ... I am the good shepherd. ... And I lay down my life for the sheep"* (John 10:10, 14–15).

When you are weary ... when it seems life isn't worth living ... when you've lost all hope, what do you need to know? You need to know the Burden-bearer—you need to know Jesus. He wants to be the Shepherd of your soul. His compassionate comfort extends to all who need rest and to all those who have lost all hope. Jesus said ...

"Come to me,
all you who are weary and burdened,
and I will give you rest."
(Matthew 11:28)

Four Points of God's Plan

#1 God's Purpose for You is *Salvation*.

What was God's motive in sending Christ to earth?

To express His love for you by saving you! The Bible says ...

"God so loved the world that he gave his one and only Son, that whoever believes in him shall not perish but have eternal life. For God did not send his Son into the world to condemn the world, but to save the world through him." (John 3:16–17)

What was Jesus' purpose in coming to earth?

To forgive your sins, to empower you to have victory over sin, and to enable you to live a fulfilled life! Jesus said ...

"I have come that they may have life, and have it to the full." (John 10:10)

#2 Your Problem is *Sin*.

What exactly is sin?

Sin is living independently of God's standard— knowing what is right, but choosing what is wrong. The Bible says ...

"Anyone, then, who knows the good he ought to do and doesn't do it, sins." (James 4:17)

What is the major consequence of sin?

Spiritual "death," eternal separation from God. Scripture states ...

"Your iniquities [sins] have separated you from your God. ... For the wages of sin is death, but the gift of God is eternal life in Christ Jesus our Lord." (Isaiah 59:2; Romans 6:23)

#3 God's Provision for You is the *Savior*.

Can anything remove the penalty for sin?

Yes! Jesus died on the cross to personally pay the penalty for your sins.

"God demonstrates his own love for us in this: While we were still sinners, Christ died for us." (Romans 5:8)

What can keep you from being separated from God?

Belief in (entrusting your life to) Jesus Christ as the only way to God the Father. Jesus says ...

"I am the way and the truth and the life. No one comes to the Father except through me." (John 14:6)

#4 Your Part is *Surrender*.

Give Christ control of your life—entrusting yourself to Him.

"Jesus said to his disciples, 'If anyone would come after me, he must deny himself and take up his cross [die to your own self-rule] and follow me. For whoever wants to save his life will lose it, but whoever loses his life for me will find it. What good will it be for a man if he gains the whole world, yet forfeits his soul?'" (Matthew 16:24–26)

Place your faith in (rely on) Jesus Christ as your personal Lord and Savior and reject your "good works" as a means of earning God's approval.

"It is by grace you have been saved, through faith—and this not from yourselves, it is the gift of God—not by works, so that no one can boast." (Ephesians 2:8–9)

The moment you choose to receive Jesus as your Lord and Savior—entrusting your life to Him—the Holy Spirit comes to live inside you. Then the Spirit gives you power to live the fulfilled life God has planned for you. If you want to be fully forgiven by God and become the person God created you to be, you can tell Him in a simple, heartfelt prayer like this:

PRAYER OF SALVATION

"God, I want a real relationship with You. I admit that many times I've chosen to go my own way instead of Your way. Please forgive me for my sins. Jesus, thank You for dying on the cross to pay the penalty for my sins. Come into my life to be my Lord and my Savior. Change me from the inside out and make me the person You created me to be. In Your holy name I pray. Amen."

STEPS TO SOLUTION

The intense battle being waged for your mind, body, soul, and spirit extends beyond a distinct line in the sand drawn between two camps. One side fights for life, bringing hope to the hopeless and engaging every resource available toward suicide prevention. The other side fights for death, enticing—even assisting—people to take their own lives, and falsely promising both a peaceful exit and a peaceful eternity.

The International Association for Suicide Prevention (IASP) is on one side of the camp, and Dignitas, a Swiss assisted suicide clinic, is on the other. The clinic's founder, Ludwig Minelli, describes suicide as a "very good possibility to escape."[27]

When you line up your thinking with God's thinking, however, you will "escape" a wrong mind-set that would keep you in bondage. Then you can say with the psalmist ...

**"You, O Lᴏʀᴅ, have delivered
my soul from death, my eyes from tears,
my feet from stumbling."
(Psalm 116:8)**

Key Verses to Memorize

Those struggling with life-threatening thoughts do not feel connected to others. They feel all alone—even alone in the midst of a crowd.

If you are now a struggler, these feelings are indeed painful, but they don't reflect God's hope for your heart. Repeat the truth of His hope every day—morning, noon, and night!

**"Find rest, O my soul,
in God alone; my hope comes from him.
He alone is my rock and my salvation;
he is my fortress, I will not be shaken."
(Psalm 62:5–6)**

Key Passage to Read

When you feel that you're drowning in the depths of despair, know that other godly people have felt the same sense of hopelessness. For example, the prophet Jeremiah emotionally "hit bottom," yet he also had the wisdom to look up to the Lord and find hope.

This passage is a step-by-step plan.

THE REMEDY TO RESTORE YOUR HOPE
LAMENTATIONS 3:19–24

▶ Remember the facts of your affliction.

"I remember my affliction and my wandering, the bitterness and the gall." (v. 19)

▶ Remember the feelings of your pain.

"I well remember them, and my soul is downcast within me." (v. 20)

▶ Recall the times when you had hope.

"Yet this I call to mind and therefore I have hope." (v. 21)

▶ Review the reward of God's love.

"Because of the Lord's great love we are not consumed, for his compassions never fail." (v. 22)

▶ Recite the fact of God's faithfulness.

"They are new every morning; great is your faithfulness." (v. 23)

▶ Rest in His fullness—He is your hope.

"I say to myself, 'The Lord is my portion; therefore I will wait for him.'" (v. 24)

When Jeremiah's thoughts led him to the deep, dark bowels of despair, he made a conscious choice to focus his mind on the love, compassion, faithfulness, and sufficiency of God. Therefore, he waited, he rested, in Him. The same choice is available to you today.

HOW TO Evaluate the Extent of the Suicidal Struggle

To determine the degree of despair, asking pertinent questions will give you much insight into the suicidal struggle.

Suicide Assessment

Initially begin with these questions about painful thoughts.

The Thoughts

▶ "Do you ever think that life is not worth living?"

▶ "Do you wish you could go to sleep and not wake up?"

▶ "Do you think about dying or wish you were dead?"

▶ "Are you thinking about harming yourself?"

▶ "Tell me more about what you are thinking."

▶ "When was the first time you had those thoughts? What was happening then?"

▶ "How long have you been thinking about taking your life?"

▶ "Have you ever thought of suicide as the ultimate revenge toward someone you resent?"

▶ "What has been happening in your life recently?"

▶ "What do you fear the most?"

▶ "How strong have these suicidal thoughts been?"

▶ "Have you talked with anyone about these thoughts?"

Job, the man God called blameless, said in the midst of his painful ordeal, *"I have no concern for myself; I despise my own life."* (Job 9:21)

The Method

▶ "Do you have a plan now?"

▶ "How would you hurt yourself?"

▶ "When do you think you would do it?"

▶ "Where would you do it?"

▶ "Do you have access to the gun/knife/intended weapon?"

▶ "Where is it? Is it locked up? Who can get to it?"

▶ "Have you already swallowed any pills/poison?"

▶ "Have you written a suicide note?"

▶ "Are you taking steps to fulfill your plan at this time?"

In his despair, Job even said, *"I prefer strangling and death, rather than this body of mine."* (Job 7:15)

Family Suicidal History

▶ "Do any of your family members suffer from a psychological illness?"

▶ "Have any of your family members been suicidal?"

▶ "Have any of your family members taken their own lives?" If yes,

▶ "Who? When?"

▶ "What were the circumstances?"

▶ "Had they received a psychiatric diagnosis?"

▶ "What impact did that have on you?"

After a family member dies of suicide, their loved ones sometimes fear that they too will be suicidal. These words spoken by Job could reflect that same fear: *"What I feared has come upon me; what I dreaded has happened to me. I have no peace, no quietness; I have no rest, but only turmoil."* (Job 3:25–26)

Personal Suicidal History

▶ "Have you ever attempted suicide in the past?"

▶ "How many times?"

▶ "When was the first time you attempted suicide?"

▶ "What was happening at that time?"

▶ "What did you do?"

▶ "When did you do it?"

▶ "How close did you come to ending your life?"

▶ "What happened after you did that?"

▶ "At that time, how much did you want to die?"

▶ "At the time, how certain were you that you would die?"

▶ "Afterward, did you feel glad or sad that you were alive?"

▶ "At the time(s), were you drinking or using drugs?"

▶ "At the time(s), what was your mood?"

▶ "Has anything changed since you tried to end your life?"

▶ "Tell me about any other times you felt suicidal."

In severe pain, Job thought back to the past: *"Why was I not hidden in the ground like a stillborn child, like an infant who never saw the light of day?"* (Job 3:16)

Medical History

▶ "How old are you?"

▶ "When was the last time you received a medical checkup?"

▶ "What was the result of the checkup?"

▶ "Have you recently had a baby?" (Checking for postpartum depression. If yes, ask about depression after the birth of any other children.)

▶ "Did you tell the doctor that you felt suicidal?"

▶ "Have you ever been to a psychologist or psychiatrist?"

▶ "Did you receive a diagnosis?"

▶ "Were you prescribed medications?"

▶ "Are you taking your medication exactly as prescribed or not really?"

Job describes the lack of meaning in his life: *"I despise my life; I would not live forever. Let me alone; my days have no meaning."* (Job 7:16)

Spiritual History

▶ "What is your religious background?"

▶ "Describe your spiritual journey."

▶ "How would you describe God? Jesus?"

▶ "What spiritual beliefs are important to you?"

▶ "Where are you spiritually?"

▶ "How do you see your relationship with God?"

▶ "Are you a member of a church? An active member of a solid, biblically based church?"

▶ "Are you involved in a small group Bible study?"

▶ "Have you shared your struggle with anyone there?"

▶ "Is someone there with whom you feel you could share this? Who?"

▶ "Would you be willing to share this?"

▶ "What would make you more hopeful about God's future, less likely to take your life, and more encouraged to keep on living?"

▶ "Do you think God cares whether you live or die?"

Though he can't seem to find the Lord, Job realizes he is not lost to the Lord. He realizes the Refiner is testing him so that he will come forth as gold.

> "He knows the way that I take; when he has tested me, I will come forth as gold. My feet have closely followed his steps; I have kept to his way without turning aside. I have not departed from the commands of his lips; I have treasured the words of his mouth more than my daily bread."
> (Job 23:10–12)

Dignitas is anything but dignified. The very existence of this clinic is a direct affront to God's plan and purpose because it encourages suicide rather than discouraging it. Dignitas is an assisted suicide clinic in Zurich, Switzerland, founded by a man who believes suicide should be available not only for the terminally ill or the severely disabled (where most in his circle draw the line), but for all people. Ludwig Minelli goes as far as to say, "We should have a nicer attitude to suicide, saying suicide is a very good possibility to escape."[28]

But while Minelli says *yes*, God says *no* to each and every thought of suicide.

Have you come to the conclusion that life is not worth living? If you've lost all desire to hope, your heavenly Father knows what you are feeling. He desires that you call out to Him. God will respond to the honest heart that offers even a flicker of willingness.

**"I call on you, O God, for you will answer me;
give ear to me and hear my prayer.
Show the wonder of your great love,
you who save by your right hand those who
take refuge in you."
(Psalm 17:6–7)**

Seven Scriptural Reasons to Say *No* to Suicide[29]

▶ **Reason #1: Suicide rejects God's offer of inner peace.**

"Do not be anxious about anything, but in everything, by prayer and petition, with thanksgiving, present your requests to God. And the peace of God, which transcends all understanding, will guard your hearts and your minds in Christ Jesus." (Philippians 4:6–7)

▶ **Reason #2: Suicide rejects God's sovereignty over the length of your life.**

"You created my inmost being; you knit me together in my mother's womb. ... Your eyes saw my unformed body. All the days ordained for me were written in your book before one of them came to be." (Psalm 139:13, 16)

▶ **Reason #3: Suicide rejects God's right to be Lord over your life.**

"Do you not know that your body is a temple of the Holy Spirit, who is in you, whom you have received from God? You are not your own." (1 Corinthians 6:19)

▶ **Reason #4: Suicide rejects God's commandment not to murder.**

"You shall not murder" (Deuteronomy 5:17).

▶ **Reason #5: Suicide rejects God's ability to heal your hurts.**

"Heal me, O LORD, and I will be healed." (Jeremiah 17:14)

▶ **Reason #6: Suicide rejects God's plan to give you hope.**

"Find rest, O my soul, in God alone; my hope comes from him." (Psalm 62:5)

▶ **Reason #7: Suicide rejects God's power already within you to make you godly.**

"His divine power has given us everything we need for life and godliness through our knowledge of him who called us by his own glory and goodness. Through these he has given us his very great and precious promises, so that through them you may participate in the divine nature and escape the corruption in the world caused by evil desires." (2 Peter 1:3–4)

Even if at times you don't want to live, all you need is the willingness to be made willing. The next time you feel despairing and disconnected, pray, *"Restore to me the joy of your salvation and grant me a willing spirit, to sustain me"* (Psalm 51:12).

Through His Spirit within you, God can empower you to choose life. Turn to Him to find the outpouring of His hope and healing—the outpouring of His compassion and comfort that you cannot generate on your own. Afterward, He will use you to rescue and help others who are struggling as you are today. See your life from God's point of view. Those who have suffered much will be used much by God. The Bible states it this way:

"The Father of compassion and the God of all comfort ... comforts us in all our troubles, So that we can comfort those in any trouble with the comfort we ourselves have received from God." (2 Corinthians 1:3–4)

Lord, Make Me *Willing*

▶ **To Be Broken**: "O God, I feel like I'm at the end. My heart is broken with despair."

- **God's Promise**: *"The sacrifices of God are a broken spirit; a broken and contrite heart ... [God] will not despise"* (Psalm 51:17).

  My Prayer: "Thank You, God, that I have reached the end of my own self-effort and I can bring You my broken heart."

▶ **To Be Yielded**: "I see no hope or no one to help me. My mind is made up—death is the only answer."

- **God's Promise**: *"Hope deferred makes the heart sick, but a longing fulfilled is a tree of life"* (Proverbs 13:12).

  My Prayer: "Thank You, God, that I can put my hope in You, the One who can fulfill my longings and give me life."

▶ **To Be Willing**: "I'm afraid to go on. I don't have the will to face the future."

- **God's Promise**: *"Do not fear, for I am with you; do not be dismayed, for I am your God. I will strengthen you and help you; I will uphold you with my righteous right hand"* (Isaiah 41:10).

  My Prayer: "Thank You, God, that through Your strength, I will turn from fear to faith—I can face the future God has for me."

▶ **To Be Assured**: "God, I feel completely alone. Nothing relieves this terrible loneliness."

- **God's Promise**: *"When you pass through the waters, I will be with you; and when you pass through the rivers, they will not sweep over you. When you walk through the fire, you will not be burned; the flames will not set you ablaze"* (Isaiah 43:2).

  My Prayer: "Thank You, God, that because of You I am never alone. Thank You for being with me even when I don't feel that You are walking with me."

▶ **To Be Guilt-free**: "I've committed too many sins. I can't be forgiven, and I don't deserve mercy."

- **God's Promise**: *"He who conceals his sins does not prosper, but whoever confesses and renounces them finds mercy"* (Proverbs 28:13).

  My Prayer: "Thank You, God, that as I confess my anger, resentment, and all of my sin, You will cleanse me."

▶ **To Be Accepting**: "I don't have the strength to accept these miserable circumstances."

- **God's Promise**: *"I can do everything through him who gives me strength"* (Philippians 4:13).

  My Prayer: "Thank You, God, for giving me the strength to accept life as it now is, and to let go of the *why*'s."

▶ **To Be Hopeful**: "Secretly, I am afraid to have hope. What if I begin to hope, but nothing really changes?"

- **God's Promise**: *"We also rejoice in our sufferings, because we know that suffering produces perseverance; perseverance, character; and character, hope. And hope does not disappoint us, because God has poured out his love into our hearts by the Holy Spirit, whom he has given us"* (Romans 5:3–5).

  My Prayer: "Thank You, God, that I can choose to put my hope in You. I will not trust in things as they seem to be, but will totally trust in You with gratitude for the unseen power of Your love."

Is your sense of hopelessness caused by unforgiveness? Have you ever said: "I have been so wronged. I know I *should* forgive, but how can I simply let my offender off the hook? I just *can't*!"? If these thoughts are driving your depression ... if these words have passed your lips or even crossed your mind, be assured you are not alone. That is precisely why you need to know that you can let go of the hurt and the heartache. You can learn ...

How to Handle "The Hook"

▶ Start by making a list of all the offenses caused by your offender.

▶ Imagine right now a meat hook around your neck and a burlap bag hanging from the hook in front of you. And imagine all the pain caused by the offenses against you—each offense on the list—dropped like rocks into the burlap bag— the bigger the offense, the bigger the rock. So, now you have 100 lbs of heavy rocks—rocks of resentment—hanging from the hook around your neck, weighing you down in despair.

▶ Ask yourself, *Do I really want to carry all that pain with me for the rest of my life?* Are you willing to take the pain from the past and release it into the hands of the Lord?

▶ If so, right now, take all the pain and release it to Jesus.

▶ Take the one who offended you off of *your* emotional hook and place your offender onto

God's hook. The Lord knows how to deal with your offender in His time and in His way. God says ...

**"It is mine to avenge; I will repay."
(Deuteronomy 32:35)**

The fact that your offender may be deceased does not mean you cannot forgive and thereby release bitterness that may have established a foothold in your heart and mind. The Bible says ...

"See to it that no one misses the grace of God and that no bitter root grows up to cause trouble and defile many." (Hebrews 12:15)

PRAYER TO FORGIVE YOUR OFFENDER

*"Lord Jesus, thank You for caring about how much my heart has been hurt.
You know the pain I have felt because of
(list every offense). Right now, I release all that pain into Your hands.
Thank You, Jesus, for dying on the cross for me and extending Your forgiveness to me.
As an act of my will, I choose to forgive
(name). Right now, I move (name) off of my emotional hook to Your hook.
I refuse all thoughts of revenge.
I trust that in Your time and in Your way You will deal with my offender as You see fit.
And Lord, thank You for giving me Your power to forgive so that I can be set free.
In Your holy name I pray. Amen."*

When you're in the darkest depths of despair, when you feel emotionally trapped with no way out, remember *you're not alone*. Countless thousands all around the world are experiencing the same feelings of hopelessness.

Besides pursuing activities that will help dissuade suicidal thoughts, reach out to others who are hurting just as you are. Find comfort and solace in sharing feelings and encouraging one another. There's no better way to bring hope and healing to yourself than by bringing hope and healing to someone else. Your own spirit will inevitably be lifted.

> **"Our hope for you is firm,**
> **because we know that**
> **just as you share in our sufferings,**
> **so also you share in our comfort."**
> **(2 Corinthians 1:7)**

If you focus on feelings of despair, then hopelessness will inevitably lead to depression and possibly to suicidal thoughts. Replace those negative, self-defeating thoughts with constructive thoughts. Occupy your mind with uplifting activities. Above all, if you are thinking about suicide, call your pastor, a suicide prevention center, a counselor, or a trusted friend. They want to help you.

Activities to Alleviate Suicidal Obsession[30]

▶ Walk, jog, bike, or swim *for physical release*

▶ Lie down or take a nap *for physical renewal*

▶ Take a long hot shower or bubble bath *for physical soothing*

▶ Curl up with a heating pad *for emotional warmth*

▶ Play with a pet or cuddle a stuffed animal *for emotional comfort*

▶ Journal or draw your feelings *for emotional release*

▶ Watch an inspiring movie *for emotional enjoyment*

▶ Play Christian praise music *for spiritual inspiration*

▶ Read a Christian book or biography *for spiritual pleasure*

▶ Memorize a verse of Scripture *for spiritual focus*

▶ Work a jigsaw or crossword puzzle *for mental stimulation*

▶ Do indoor or outdoor chores *to remove clutter*

▶ Clean a refrigerator, cabinet, closet, or a drawer *to feel productive*

▶ Prepare a grocery list, selecting healthy foods *to meet physical needs*

- ▶ Organize coupons and go shopping *to meet practical needs*

- ▶ Take prescription medicine as needed *to meet medical needs*

- ▶ Go to the park and watch the people *to enjoy others*

- ▶ Sort through clothes to give to the needy *to benefit others*

- ▶ Volunteer at a ministry, church, or charity *to serve others*

- ▶ Call a friend and offer help *to reach out to others*

> **"There is surely a future hope for you, and your hope will not be cut off."**
> **(Proverbs 23:18)**

HOW TO Hold On to the Lifeline of Hope

God's Word emphasizes the importance of belonging to and attending a supportive and encouraging church. That means gathering regularly with a group of people who can love you and encourage you. There's a community of people near you who need you as much as you need them. The Bible gives this message of encouragement: *"Let us not give up meeting together, as some are in the habit of doing, but let us encourage one another"* (Hebrews 10:25).

Then, if you begin to feel like you're drowning in waves of despair, when you're at your darkest moment of desperation, you'll have people you can contact, people who will connect with you, who truly care when you're in crisis. You are not alone. Let God love you through His people.

> **"May the Lord make your love increase**
> **and overflow for each other**
> **and for everyone else."**
> **(1 Thessalonians 3:12)**

Crisis Card

How can you be rescued in an ocean of despair? You need to be prepared *before* you are overwhelmed by wave upon wave of hopelessness. With or without the help of others, you can equip yourself *ahead of time* by making a *Lifeline Crisis Card*.

From the following suggestions, ***choose what is appropriate for you,*** then outline the steps you will take when you find yourself in an emotional crisis. Give a copy of your plan to trusted family members or friends, and keep a copy with you at all times—in your wallet, car, desk, medicine cabinet, and kitchen cupboard. When you first begin to feel your heart sinking: *Reach out for your lifeline!*

> **"Guard my life and rescue me;**
> **let me not be put to shame,**
> **for I take refuge in you."**
> **(Psalm 25:20)**

▶ **When in crisis, I will focus on God.**

- I will pray:

  "In you, O Lord, I have taken refuge; let me never be put to shame; deliver me in your righteousness. Turn your ear to me, come quickly to my rescue; be my rock of refuge, a strong fortress to save me. Since you are my rock and my fortress, for the sake of your name lead and guide me" (Psalm 31:1–3; pray verses 1–9, 14–24).

- I will recite Scriptures aloud:

  "Have mercy on me, O God, have mercy on me, for in you my soul takes refuge. I will take refuge in the shadow of your wings until the disaster has passed." (Psalm 57:1; also read Psalms 27 and 28)

- I will claim God's promises:

  "My comfort in my suffering is this: Your promise preserves my life." (Psalm 119:50)

- I will consider how special it is to be a child of God:

  "How great is the love the Father has lavished on us, that we should be called children of God! And that is what we are!" (1 John 3:1)

▶ **When in crisis, I will listen to Christian praise music and Scripture songs.**

"Sing to the Lord, you saints of his; praise his holy name. … Weeping may remain for a night, but rejoicing comes in the morning." (Psalm 30:4–5)

- I won't listen to heavy metal or acid rock.

- I won't listen to rap or hip hop.

- I won't listen to sad, country-western music.

▶ **When in crisis, I will question myself.**

- "Why do I feel the need to hurt myself?"

- "What do I think I will accomplish through this?"

- "According to God, is what I am telling myself the truth or a lie?"

- "Are my actions and desires reflecting my true identity in Christ, or are they coming out of my past experiences?"

- "What effect would harming myself have on those who care about me?"

"Surely you desire truth in the inner parts; you teach me wisdom in the inmost place." (Psalm 51:6)

▶ **When in crisis, I will make positive affirmations.**

- "My life is worth living because His Word assures me that I am a child of God."

- "God loves me and has a purpose for my life."

- "Because God has a plan for me, I will treat the body He gave me with respect."

- "Even though I can't see the future, I will walk by faith, not by sight."

"Whatever is true, whatever is noble, whatever is right, whatever is pure, whatever is lovely, whatever is admirable—if anything is excellent or praiseworthy—think about such things." (Philippians 4:8)

▶ When in crisis, I will review encouraging words.

- Read aloud positive letters and notes from friends and family.

- Review positive thoughts of why it's worth it to heal.

- Recall those who believe in me and in my growth.

- Remember what others have said about why there is hope for me.

- Rehearse God's promise:

"The LORD himself goes before you and will be with you; he will never leave you nor forsake you. Do not be afraid; do not be discouraged." (Deuteronomy 31:8)

▶ When in crisis, I will not:

- Act on impulse

- Do any harmful act or anything even potentially harmful to myself, to others, or to property

- Drive my automobile if there is a possibility of my driving recklessly

- Act rashly

"God has not given us a spirit of fear, but of power and of love and of a sound mind." (2 Timothy 1:7 NKJV)

▶ **When in doubt as to whether an action is harmful, I will ask myself:**

- "Would God approve of this?"

- "Would the people I love approve of this?"

- "Would the people who care about me approve of this?"

If the answer is *NO,* then I must not do it! If I would hurt innocent people whom I care about, then I must not do it! No rationalizations, no excuses, just *Do Not Do It!*

"You need to persevere so that when you have done the will of God, you will receive what he has promised." (Hebrews 10:36)

▶ **When in crisis, I will:**

- Make a list of names and phone numbers of people I can call for help.

- Make copies of my list and put them in strategic places (bedside table, medicine cabinet, file cabinet, desk drawer, car).

- Give my list to several caring people.

- After going through the previous steps—if I am still in a crisis—I will reach out and call others who will be helpful and truthful. (They can help me regain perspective.) I will continue to go down my call list until I have reached someone.

- State directly, "I am calling because I am in an emotional crisis." I will honestly discuss the feelings and events that led to the crisis and will explore possible solutions.

- Continue to make phone calls, including call backs, until the crisis is resolved, no matter what time of day or night.

Friend: _____

Relative: _____

Friend: _____

Relative: _____

Friend: _____

Therapist: _____

Doctor: _____

Church: _____

Pastor: _____

Crisis Hot Line: _____

Suicide Prevention Hotline: **1-800-Suicide (784-2433)**

**"Two are better than one, because they
have a good return for their work:
If one falls down, his friend can help him up.
But pity the man who falls
and has no one to help him up!"
(Ecclesiastes 4:9–10)**

▶ If still in crisis after completing these steps:

- I will ensure my physical and emotional safety by going to a safe environment where I am not alone.

- I will make arrangements to be with a friend or supportive person.

- I will go to a public place where harming myself is difficult.

- If all else fails, I will go to a hospital emergency room and tell them, "I am at risk of harming myself." I will make it clear, "I do not want to check in—I simply want to sit in the waiting room for a little while so that I won't act on my impulses."

- If I have diligently and honestly worked through these steps and I'm still in trouble, then I'm truly in a crisis situation that may require hospitalization for my protection.

"Listen to advice and accept instruction, and in the end you will be wise." (Proverbs 19:20)

Say to yourself, "I can make it safely through a crisis. In God's eyes I am valuable, and my life and safety are important!" No matter how painful your ordeal, no matter the hurt that you feel, God knows. God hears. God cares.

"You hear, O LORD, the desire of the afflicted; you encourage them, and you listen to their cry. ... He will respond to the prayer of the destitute; he will not despise their plea." (Psalm 10:17; 102:17)

The most essential lifeline you can provide to a suicidal struggler is HOPE. Even if you feel inadequate to become involved with someone who is suicidal, God may draw you into that person's life to be a reflection of His love. Consider such a divine encounter to be a candle of hope to someone living in darkness. Jesus said ...

"Let your light shine before men, that they may see your good deeds and praise your Father in heaven." (Matthew 5:16)

Where There's Life, There's HOPE!

"We have this hope as an anchor for the soul, firm and secure." (Hebrews 6:19)

Honestly Confront

▶ Take all talk of death and suicide seriously. Repeat back what was said: *"I'm hearing you say life's not worth living. Is that right?"*

▶ Identify with their pain and express your concern. *"That must feel painfully empty. I want you to know I care about your pain!"*

▶ Ask these direct questions: *"Are you thinking about harming yourself? How? Do you have a plan?"*

▶ Seek to find out what problem is causing the pain. Ask, *"What has been so painful that you don't want to live?"*

The Bible explains this compassionate approach:

> **"The purposes of a man's heart are deep waters, but a man of understanding draws them out."**
> **(Proverbs 20:5)**

Offer Options

▶ Acknowledge the fact that life is hard.

▶ Point out that choices in life often consist of unpleasant possibilities.

▶ List possible options on a sheet of paper.

▶ Rank the options in order of preference.

▶ Communicate God's purposes for suffering. One purpose, for example, is to develop compassion: *"Many people are hurting just like you are. They feel desperately alone, assuming that no one understands their pain. You know what it's like to hurt. Your personal pain enables you to have a ministry of compassion. You are being prepared right now to be a lifeline of hope for someone else who feels hopeless."* When you speak with kindness and compassion, you reflect the wisdom of God's Word.

> **"As God's chosen people, holy and dearly loved, clothe yourselves with compassion, kindness, humility, gentleness and patience."**
> **(Colossians 3:12)**

PRESENT A CONTRACT (SEE PAGE 81)

▶ Build a relationship by showing your care and willingness to help.

▶ Ask if the person would be willing to make a contract with you. *"Will you promise that if you are considering harming yourself, you will call me before doing anything?"*

▶ Be sure to obtain a signature.

▶ Make a commitment to stay in contact.

"Carry each other's burdens, and in this way you will fulfill the law of Christ."
(Galatians 6:2)

ENLIST HELP

▶ Encourage the person to have a physical checkup.

▶ Seek a trained counselor or therapist.

▶ Call a minister.

▶ Contact the Suicide Crisis Center in your city (area).

▶ Help make arrangements for hospitalization.

"Plans fail for lack of counsel,
but with many advisers they succeed."
(Proverbs 15:22)

My Contract of HOPE

The following is a solemn binding contract. This contract cannot be declared null and void without the written agreement of both parties.

I promise that if I should consider harming myself, I will talk with you before I do anything destructive.

I sign my name as a pledge of my integrity.

Signature _____

Date _____

Signature _____

Date _____

"Anyone who is among the living has hope."
(Ecclesiastes 9:4)

Sworn to Secrecy

QUESTION: "I promised I would keep my friend's secret about suicide. If I tell, am I breaking the right to privacy?"

ANSWER: Never keep any possibility of suicide a secret. Take your friend's suicidal words seriously. You are not betraying your friend. In fact, you may be the only one in a position to help save the life of your friend.

▶ Say, "I didn't realize that what I was promising could actually hurt you. I care about you too much to keep that promise."

▶ Encourage your friend to tell a responsible adult and seek professional help.

▶ Talk to an adult whom you trust *immediately* if you feel the risk is imminent!

Realize, saving a life is always more important than keeping a secret. You may risk losing your friendship by breaking your promise, but keeping your promise and then losing your friend would be a far greater tragedy.

The Bible says ...

"We who are strong ought to bear with the failings of the weak and not to please ourselves." (Romans 15:1)

Tragically, those who take their lives fail to move from destructive to productive thinking. They fail to realize that *now is not forever*. They fail to see that *suicide is a permanent reaction to a temporary problem*.

One fact about life as we know it is that it is constantly changing; people and circumstances are constantly changing. Just as the seasons of the year change, the seasons of life change. *Now is not forever! Now is not forever!* In His time, God can and will change your circumstances and—if you let Him—He will change your heart. Like David, you can one day say ...

> "To you, O LORD, I called; to the Lord I cried for mercy. ... You turned my wailing into dancing; you removed my sackcloth and clothed me with joy, that my heart may sing to you and not be silent. O LORD my God, I will give you thanks forever." (Psalm 30:8, 11–12)

Reasonable Responses to Suicidal Statements

When first responding to suicidal statements, don't *counter*—instead *connect*. Don't focus on countering with your points, but rather connecting with the person. Then, through the relationship, you *"earn the right"* to be heard.

▶ **"There is nothing left in life I care about. It's pointless to go on living."**

"I know your present pain is overshadowing everything dear to you right now. Tell me, please, what you have cared about up to now that has made life meaningful for you. Are there other things you could care about if your pain were not so great?"

▶ **"I can't face the future. The only thing to do is just escape it all."**

"I hear your desperation, and I know the future can sometimes seem impossible to bear. Tell me what the future holds that you think you can't face. And talk to me about some of the fearful challenges you have already faced and conquered that seemed insurmountable at the time."

▶ **"Things will never change. Death would be better than this."**

"I definitely agree with you that there are things in everyone's life that will never change. But that doesn't mean we can't figure out a way to change the degree of their impact on us. Would you be willing for us to talk about the things in your life that you want to change and then explore ways to diminish their control over your life?"

▶ **"I may as well end it all. I don't matter anyway."**

"You certainly matter a lot to me, and it hurts my heart that you feel so defeated and down on yourself. What would it take to make you feel valuable—to let you know that your life has meaning?"

▶ **"It won't really hurt anyone else. Actually, I'll be doing everyone a favor."**

"Well, I'm already hurting just knowing you are hurting so badly. It is heartbreaking to me tha you feel so uncared for that you actually think no one would be hurt by your death and that you would be doing everyone a favor. What has caused you to come to such a drastic conclusion? What could the people who love you have done that you would feel this way about them?"

▶ **"I've done all that can be done. There is only one thing left to do."**

"I can hear your discouragement in your voice, and I am sorry. Please tell me what you are referring to and what you have hoped to accomplish by your efforts. Maybe between the two of us we can come up with another way of looking at it and hopefully gain a new perspective."

▶ **"Soon it will be all over, and then I will have peace!"**

"You sound really tired and exhausted and just ready to give up. Would you share with me what it is that has worn you out and robbed you of your peace? What does the peace you are wanting look like to you? How did you attain peace in the past, and how did you come to lose it?"

▶ **"I can't go on living like this. Life is hopeless."**

"You sound like you have really come to the end of your resources and are in desperate need of a drastic change in your life. What is making life seem so unbearable? What has led you to conclude that life is hopeless? What would have to happen for you to have hope?"

▶ **"I'm too depressed to go on."**

"I know life seems hopeless right now and you don't feel like you have the strength to keep on keeping on. If I could, I'd pour my own strength into you but I can't. All I can do is remind you that each day you work to get better will bring you another day closer to conquering the mountain you are climbing. And I can be here as a constant reminder that you are not alone and that you are loved more than words can ever express. Together with the Lord, we can and we will meet this challenge. We will experience *'the goodness of the Lord in the land of the living'*" (Psalm 27:13).

▶ **"Everyone will understand. I have suffered long enough."**

"I understand your wanting the suffering to stop. I have no doubt that everyone who loves you hates to see you suffer and would take it from you if they could. But taking your life will bring suffering to them, and I know you don't want to do that."

▶ **"Everyone has given up on me, so I'm giving up on me!"**

"I realize you feel that you cannot change, and it seems easier to just give up than to keep on trying. But I know everyone hasn't given up on you because I haven't given up on you. I'm sure there are others who feel the same as I feel about you. You may not yet be the person you want to be, but you can become that person by taking just one step at a time. Let's look for a possible s you can take today."

Unless hopeless words are replaced with   peful words and those who feel disconnected from others feel reconnected, those who have lost hope will come to the conclusion that death is the only possible solution to their problems. This is a lie! Satan is the father of lies and the author of such fatal thinking. Ultimately, suicide is a deliberate choice to believe the enemy's twisted reasoning: that taking your own life is the most reasonable way out. Jesus said of Satan ...

> **"He was a murderer from the beginning, not holding to the truth, for there is no truth in him. When he lies, he speaks his native language, for he is a liar and the father of lies." (John 8:44)**

"To be, or not to be, that is the question."[31] Or to put it another way: To live or to die ... which is better? That is the *fictional* question posed by Shakespeare in his centuries-old tragedy *Hamlet*.

The answer to that question goes back much further in time and is spoken by God Himself.

> **"I have set before you life and death. ... Now choose life." (Deuteronomy 30:19)**

Life without Christ is a hopeless end.
Life with Christ is an endless hope.
CHOOSE LIFE!

—June Hunt

SCRIPTURES TO MEMORIZE

I don't **see the goodness of the Lord**. How can I have the **heart** to keep on **living**?

> *"I am still confident of this: **I will see the goodness of the Lord** in the land of the **living**. Wait for the Lord; be strong and take **heart** and wait for the Lord."* (Psalm 27:13–14)

I feel alone, **brokenhearted**, and **crushed in spirit**. Where is **the Lord** in all this?

> *"**The Lord** is close to the **brokenhearted** and saves those who are **crushed in spirit**."* (Psalm 34:18)

My soul is **downcast** and **so disturbed**. Where can I find **hope**?

> *"Why are you **downcast**, O **my soul**? Why **so disturbed** within me? Put your **hope** in God, for I will yet praise him, my Savior and my God."* (Psalm 43:5)

My pain is beyond my **own understanding**. Why should I **trust** anyone with my **heart**?

> *"**Trust** in the Lord with all your **heart** and lean not on your **own understanding**; in all your ways acknowledge him, and he will make your paths straight."* (Proverbs 3:5–6)

My life is filled with **fear**. Can anyone **strengthen and help** me?

> *"Do not **fear**, for I am with you; do not be dismayed, for I am your God. I will **strengthen** you **and help** you; I will uphold you with my righteous right hand."* (Isaiah 41:10)

My **body** is my **own**. I'm under no obligation to **honor God** with it. If I want to destroy it—isn't that my right?

> *"Do you not know that your **body** is a temple of the Holy Spirit, who is in you, whom you have received from God? You are not your **own**; you were bought at a price. Therefore **honor God** with your body."* (1 Corinthians 6:19–20)

I don't have any **hope**. Can anyone **give** me help with **plans** for the **future**?

> *"'I know the **plans** I have for you,' declares the Lord, 'plans to prosper you and not to harm you, plans to **give** you **hope** and a **future**.'"* (Jeremiah 29:11)

I feel **pressed on every side**. How can I *not* have **despair**?

> *"We are hard **pressed on every side**, but not crushed; perplexed, but not in **despair**; persecuted, but not abandoned; struck down, but not destroyed."* (2 Corinthians 4:8–9)

How can I go on **living**? My life **has** no **hope**.

> *"Anyone who is among the **living has hope**."* (Ecclesiastes 9:4)

NOTES

1. World Health Organization, "The World Health Report 2004" (Geneva, Switzerland: WHO, 2004), http://www. who.int/whr/2004/annex/topic/en/annex_2_en.pdf.

2. World Health Organization, "Suicide Prevention (SUPRE)" (Geneva, Switzerland: WHO, 2009), http:// www.who.int/mental_health/prevention/suicide/ suicideprevent/en/.

3. The categories in this section are unique, for elaboration on Emile Durkheim's suicide categories (egoistic, altruistic, and anomic see John H. Hewett, *After Suicide*, Christian Care Books, ed. Wayne E. Oates (Philadelphia, PA: Westminster, 1980), 28–29; Theodore M. Johnson, "Suicide," in *Baker Encyclopedia of Psychology*, edited by David G. Benner (Grand Rapids: Baker, 1987), 1130–1133; John White, *The Masks of Melancholy: A Christian Physician Looks at Depression & Suicide* (Downers Grove, IL: InterVarsity, 1982), 150–153.

4. Hewett, *After Suicide*, 30; H. Norman Wright, *Crisis Counseling: What to Do and Say During the First 72 Hours*, Updated and expanded ed. (Ventura, CA: Regal, 1993), 128.

5. Flavius Josephus, *The Wars of the Jews*, trans. William Whiston (Peabody, MA: Hendrickson, 1987), book 7, chapters 8–9.

6. Wesley J. Smith, "Australia's Dr. Death: Spreading the Assisted-Suicide Gospel," *National Review Online*, (New York: National Review, November 26, 2002), http://www.nationalreview.com/comment/comment-smith112602.asp.

7. E.S. Schneidman, "Suicide" *Comprehensive Textbook of Psychiatry*, ed. A.M. Freedman, H.I. Kaplan, and B.J. Sadock (Baltimore: Williams & Wilkins Co., 1975), 1774–1785; see also Hewett, *After Suicide*, 23–28, 91–96; White, *The Masks of Melancholy*, 164–167.

8. Centers for Disease Control and Prevention, "Holiday Suicides: Fact or Myth? (Atlanta: Centers for Disease Control, 2009), http://www.cdc.gov/ViolencePrevention/suicide/holiday.html.

9. American Foundation for Suicide Prevention, "Reporting on Suicide: Recommendations for the Media" (New York: American Foundation for Suicide Prevention, 2010), http://www.afsp.org/index.cfm?fuseaction=home.viewPage&page_id=7852EBBC-9FB2-6691-54125A1AD4221E49.

10. American Foundation for Suicide Prevention, "Facts and Figures" (New York: American Foundation for Suicide Prevention, 2006), http://www.afsp.org/index.cfm?fuseaction=home.viewpage&page_id=050FEA9F-B064-4092-B1135C3A70DE1FDA.

11. Archibald Hart and Catherine Hart Weber, *Unveiling Depression in Women: A Practical Guide to Understanding and Overcoming Depression* (Grand Rapids: Fleming H. Revell, 2002), 56.

12. Tony Dungy with Nathan Whitaker, *Quiet Strength: A Memoir* (Carol Stream, Illinois: Tyndale House, 2007), for James Dungy's death, see 248–256.

13. Dungy, *Quiet Strength*, 254.

14. Vern R. Andress, "The Crisis of Suicide," *Ministry: International Journal for Pastors*, vol. 69, no. 7 (Hagerstown, MD: Seventh-day Adventist Ministerial Association, July 1996), 19–20.

15. American Academy of Child & Adolescent Psychiatry, "Facts for Families: Teen Suicide" (n.p.: American Academy of Child & Adolescent Psychiatry, 2008), http://www.aacap.org/cs/root/facts_for_families/teen_suicide.

16. World Health Organization, "Suicide Prevention," 2009, http://www.who.int/mental_health/prevention/suicide/suicideprevent/en/.

17. James L. Levenson, ed., *The American Psychiatric Publishing Textbook of Psychosomatic Medicine*, 1st ed. (Arlington, VA: American Psychiatric Publishing, Inc., 2005), 221.

18. James A. Dosman, and Donald W. Cockcroft, *Principles of Health and Safety in Agriculture* (Boca Raton, FL: CRC Press, 1989), 385.

19. Andress, "The Crisis of Suicide," *Ministry: International Journal for Pastors*, vol. 69, no. 7, 19.

20. Levenson, ed., *The American Psychiatric Publishing Textbook of Psychosomatic Medicine*, 1st ed., 221.

21. World Health Organization, "Suicide Prevention," 2009, http://www.who.int/mental_health/prevention/suicide/suicideprevent/en/.

22. Natalie Staats and Mark Dombeck, "Suicide Statistics" (Columbus, OH: MentalHealth.net, 2007), http://www.mentalhelp.net/poc/view_doc.php?type=doc&id=13737.

23. Vladeta Ajdacic-Gross, Mitchell G. Weiss, Mariann Ring, Urs Hepp, Matthias Bopp, Felix Gutzwiller, Wulf Rossler, "Methods of Suicide: International Suicide Patterns Derived from the WHO Mortality Database," *Bulletins of the World Health Organization*, vol. 86, no. 9 (Geneva, Switzerland: WHO, September 2008), http://www.who.int/bulletin/volumes/86/9/07-043489/en/index.html.

24. Leo Lewis, "Japan Gripped by Suicide Epidemic," *The TimesOnline*, June 19, 2008, http://www.timesonline.co.uk/tol/news/world/asia/article4170649.ece.

25. Henri Blocher, translated by Roger Van Dyk, *Suicide* (Downer's Grove, IL: InterVarsity, 1972) 5, 7.

26. National Institute of Mental Health, "The Numbers Count: Mental Disorders in America" (Bethesda, MD: US Department of Health and Human Services, 2010) http://www.nimh.nih.gov/health/publications/the-numbers-count-mental-disorders-in-america/index.shtml#ConwellSuiAging.

27. David Brown, "Dignitas Founder Plans Assisted Suicide of Healthy Woman," *The TimesOnline,* April 3, 2009, http://www.timesonline.co.uk/tol/news/world/europe/article6021947.ece.

28. Brown, "Dignitas Founder Plans Assisted Suicide of Healthy Woman."

29. Rus Walton, *Biblical Solutions to Contemporary Problems* (Bentwood, TN: Wolgemuth & Hyatt, 1988), 305–307.

30. For additional activities see Melody Beattie, ed., *A Reason to Live* (Wheaton, IL: Tyndale House, 1991), 15–79.

31. *Hamlet* by William Shakespeare in Kenneth Branagh, *Hamlet: Screenplay, Introduction, and Film Diary* (New York: W.W. Norton & Company, 1996), 77.

June Hunt's HOPE FOR THE HEART booklets are biblically-based, and full of practical advice that is relevant, spiritually-fulfilling and wholesome. Each topic presents scriptural truths and examples of real-life situations to help readers relate and integrate June's counseling guidance into their own lives. Practical for individuals from all walks of life, this new booklet series invites readers into invaluable restoration, emotional health, and spiritual freedom.

HOPE FOR THE HEART TITLES

Adultery	ISBN 9781596366848
Alcohol & Drug Abuse	ISBN 9781596366596
Anger	ISBN 9781596366411
Codependency	ISBN 9781596366510
Conflict Resolution	ISBN 9781596366473
Confrontation	ISBN 9781596366886
Considering Marriage	ISBN 9781596366763
Decision Making	ISBN 9781596366541
Depression	ISBN 9781596366497
Domestic Violence	ISBN 9781596366824
Fear	ISBN 9781596366701
Forgiveness	ISBN 9781596366435
Gambling	ISBN 9781596366862
Grief	ISBN 9781596366572
Guilt	ISBN 9781596366961
Hope	ISBN 9781596366558
Loneliness	ISBN 9781596366909
Manipulation	ISBN 9781596366749
Parenting	ISBN 9781596366725
Rejection	ISBN 9781596366787
Self-Worth	ISBN 9781596366695
Sexual Integrity	ISBN 9781596366947
Success Through Failure	ISBN 9781596366923
Suicide Prevention	ISBN 978159636680C
Verbal & Emotional Abuse	ISBN 97815963664⁵

www.aspirepress.com

The HOPE FOR THE HEART Biblical Counseling Library is Your Solution!

- Easy-to-read, perfect for anyone.
- Short. Only 92 pages. Good for the busy person.
- Christ-centered biblical advice and practical help
- Tested and proven over 20 years of June Hunt's radio ministry
- 25 titles in the series – each tackling a key issue people face today.
- Affordable. You or your church can give away, lend, or sell them.

Display available for churches and ministries.

www.aspirepress.com